OVERCOME BARRIERS

By Susan Scoggins

LEGAL DISCLAIMER:

The Publisher has strived to be as accurate and complete as possible in the creation of this report, even though he does not warrant or represent at any time that the contents within are accurate due to the rapidly changing nature of the Internet.

Any viewed slights of specific persons, individuals, or companies are unintended. The purpose of this book is to educate, and there are no guarantees of income, sales or results implied. The publisher/author/reseller can, for that reason, not be held accountable for any bad results you may attain when implementing the methods or when following any standards set out for you in this book.

The author and publisher shall have neither liability nor responsibility to any person or entity concerning any loss or damage caused or alleged to be caused directly or indirectly by this book

INTRODUCTION

Scrolling through social media, you likely see lots of picture-perfect lives that do not match your own. When scrolling, you likely feel your life doesn't compare to others', specifically when a difficulty or difficulty comes your way.

I'm going to let you in on a little trick, however. Everybody faces challenges. Whether they pick to share those obstacles for other people to see is up to them. Instead of residence on comparing your barriers to others, it's most valuable to focus on yourself, gear your frame of mind to get rid of the obstacle and turn it into success.

But how does one do that? Many challenges feel challenging and difficult to beat. As a result, it is simple to end up being disillusioned or give up on the barrier altogether. Or, like some individuals, you might get resentful of others who appear to conquer any obstacle and turn it into success with ease.

Both quitting and animosity are worthless. By altering your mindset, you can end up being somebody who turns obstacles into success. Do not get me wrong, it will take a great deal of hard work, determination, and blood, sweat, and tears, but you too can overcome any barriers and transform them into success.

In this book, we're going to inform you how to do it. We start by taking a look at what barriers are and how you should perceive them. From there, we take a look at important points like why understanding matters and the level of control you have over obstacles. These first few chapters are essential for setting a solid structure for getting rid of challenges.

Next, we provide you the two essential steps for actively overcoming your barriers, including identifying them and setting objectives for direct action.

Finally, we end by discussing the value of concentrating on yourself, psychological durability, and continued practice.

Together, these chapters give you an essential plan for not just conquering one challenge in your life but how to gain from your challenges so that you can turn any obstacle you deal with into success. Whether you are facing a major barrier at this moment or wish too much better your life, utilize this book as a guide for transforming any difficulty into a success. Let's start.

CHAPTER 1

THE TRUTH ABOUT OBSTACLES

Before jumping into how to get rid of obstacles, you require to understand the truth of them. Everybody understands what a challenge is, but most have an impractical and warped concept about it. Instead of viewing obstacles as opportunities for growth, individuals see them as occasions working against them. This unrealistic idea makes it far more difficult to conquer your challenge and change it into success.

With that in mind, you need to know the fact about barriers: challenges are not all bad. I understand this idea might sound a little radical, but it holds. Similar to everything else in life, obstacles come with both positives and negatives. Recognizing both sides will assist you to overcome the obstacle rapidly and efficiently.

Why Looking at Both the Negatives and Positives Matters

Whenever a barrier comes your way, it is essential to keep in mind this fact. If you just focus on the negatives, which the majority of people do, it is much easier to get distraught, overloaded, and depressed by the circumstance. This will make it more challenging to overcome the challenge and turn it into success.

However, if you look at the negatives and the positives, you see the challenge in a lot more reasonable light. This sensible understanding of obstacles enables you to think reasonably and plainly about the task at hand. From there, you can start to conquer your obstacle instead of getting overwhelmed by it.

Not to mention, you remove the majority of the negatives of challenges whenever you view the positives. This will make it a lot easier and more satisfying to fight your challenges, even if you aren't always succeeding as quickly as you would like.

Possible Negatives of Obstacles

Challenges include several negatives. Even though you shouldn't get captured in the negatives, you ought to be aware of them so that you know how to best go about your situation and get rid of the obstacle. Whenever you understand the negatives, more of the power is returned to you.

As a result, you can begin to master the barrier because the negatives are your own. Acknowledging them just makes them less frightening. The specific negatives of the challenge will depend on the challenge. For example, your challenge might be discovering a brand-new task. In this case, the negatives might be that you are under monetary tension, require to move, or something else related to the real task. These negatives are different from the negatives of various obstacles, like relationship difficulties.

In addition to the challenge-focused negatives, some negatives prevail in all obstacles. Most especially, obstacles need you to work. If you already have a full-time task and other responsibilities, the included obligation of getting rid of the barrier can take a great deal of your time and energy, even for the most hardworking of people.

Not just that, but barriers challenge you physically, mentally, and emotionally. Each time you find yourself in a brand-new barrier, you are required to challenge yourself to grow as a person. This procedure uses up, once again, a lot of energy, and it can bring up a lot of negative emotions depending on the scenario.

The needed effort and emotional turmoil that include the majority of barriers are what make obstacles so terrible. Most people don't like extra work. So, they grow to dislike barriers.

Ensured Positives of Obstacles

In addition to the negatives, obstacles have a lot of positives. The majority of people stop working to see these positives, and they concentrate on the negatives rather. Though this is extremely appealing to do, you ought to try your hardest to keep the positives in your mind. The positives will assist you to get rid of the challenges, remain encouraged, and take pleasure in the process.

Forces You to Grow

The biggest favorable of any challenge is that it challenges you to grow. Even though obstacles come with a great deal of hard work and effort, it is the only way for you to become the person you want to be. In other words, difficulties make you a better individual.

Some challenges may make you physically better, such as unmatched health care, while others will make you emotionally more durable. It doesn't matter how the challenge makes you grow. What matters is that you grow and become a much better individual at the end of all of it.

Helps You to Get to Know Yourself Better

Another advantage to coming out of barriers is that you are familiar with yourself better. We are frequently trained to get to know our colleagues, relative, and pals, however, we typically forget to understand ourselves. This makes it more difficult for us to trust our thoughts and understand what we want out of life.

Obstacles require us to reflect on ourselves and the world. It teaches us our strengths, weak points, and limitations. This allows us to learn more about ourselves in such a way that would not be possible without challenges.

Enhances Self-Esteem

As we grow and learn more about ourselves much better, our self-esteem grows also. So, challenges result in increased self-esteem, which is their third benefit. Self-confidence is what helps us to understand our value outside of our accomplishments and skills. It is necessary for a delighted and working life.

Improves Relationships

The last benefit of challenges is that they can enhance our relationships. You likely have seen that individuals with shared hardships tend to be some of your strongest and most relied on relationships. As you go through challenges, you end up being more understanding and able to communicate with other people in similar situations.

Recap

All in all, challenges are not an entirely bad thing. Even though they are a lot of work and can put stress on your life, they force you to grow, help you to be familiar with yourself, improve your self-esteem, and improve your relationships. Remembering these positives and the negatives will help you get rid of the challenge because of your sensible and logical frame of mind.

CHAPTER 2

PERCEPTION MATTERS

Something that we discussed in the last chapter however didn't explicitly discuss is the problem of perception. Our understandings are how we interpret occasions or individuals based upon our sensory experiences. Even though our perceptions are all we understand, how we perceive an occasion may not be precise to how it unfolds in reality.

Most likely enough, we can never leave our understandings, no matter how hard we attempt. Understandings alter every single element of our everyday life. How we view the world eventually identifies a number of our situations and feelings.

Because of how essential understanding is in our life, your perception of the obstacle will mostly identify how you manage it and whether you can overcome it. Enhance your perception of obstacles to assist you to turn any challenge into a success.

What the Psychology States About Understanding

Psychology has done a great deal of research study on understanding. As we already pointed out, psychology figures out that our understanding is determined by our sensory experience with the world, implying our sense of sight, smell, touch, and more.

More so, psychology has discovered that it determines how we react to our obstacles. For example, if we adversely view obstacles, we are more likely to give up and feel defeated by them. On the other hand, having an optimistic mindset about the obstacle makes us more likely to get rid of the challenge and prosper.

The most helpful thing that psychology informs us about perception is that we have some control. Though it is impossible to have complete control, we can a little alter our understandings by paying attention, purposefully turning our understanding into significance, acting accordingly, and practicing with our new frame of mind.

- Pay attention: What is your perception of an event? How does it differ from reality? How do you understand?

- Give your understanding significance: What does it indicate to you? Do you agree with this significance? Should you change the meaning?

- Act accordingly: How do my actions reflect my view of the circumstance?

- Practice: What are manner ins which I can include this new state of mind into my everyday life?

What this means for challenges is that you can turn your unfavorable perception or frame of mind into a favorable one. Just with deliberate and dedicated action, you can find yourself more likely to prosper by altering your mindset.

As you are actively attempting to alter your mindset, it is best to measure your progress by taking notes or using some app. Continue to act by this brand-new frame of mind and track your progress. Stay optimistic even when it's difficult, and you will begin to see your state of a mind shift.

Popular Mindsets

Considering that understanding matters, you are probably questioning what sort of a mindset you must have. There are three popular states of mind, however only one will result in long-term success. The fixed frame of mind, the blended frame of mind, and the growth state of mind are all 3 popular frames of mind that people unwittingly have.

Fixed State of mind

The fixed state of mind informs us that we are born with skills and abilities. We can not truly surpass our talents, implying our success is completely as much as our genetics. For instance, a fixed mindset would inform you that you can never get a good grade in school considering that you are not smart.

This mindset is incredibly popular, however, it is harmful. It removes any power over our situations and blames it on our natural abilities. Not just that, but the repaired state of mind is false. In the example pointed out in the last paragraph, a student presumes they can never get a good grade since they are not wise. Except for extreme learning disabilities, most trainees can get a good grade with hard work and effort, even if they aren't the most naturally intelligent. This shows the fixed frame of mind to be incorrect.

Development State of mind

The reverse of the repaired state of mind is the growth frame of mind. The growth state of mind tells you that you have certain natural capabilities and strengths, however, you can nurture your weak points and grow as a person. For example, a growth state of mind might inform you that you aren't the greatest at mathematics, but you can enhance with commitment and hard work.

The growth mindset is by far the very best frame of mind for conquering challenges and becoming effective. It prevents you from becoming overloaded and giving up when confronted with a new difficulty. Instead, it helps you to remain concentrated and determined to enhance yourself.

If you wish to conquer any obstacle, you need to start moving your state of mind from a repaired one to a growth variation.

Blended State of mind

In the process of shifting from a fixed mindset to a growth one, you will likely find yourself with a blended state of mind. A blended frame of mind is one that remains in between a fixed and development one. Sometimes, you will find yourself thinking in fixed terms, but you will find yourself believing in growth terms at other times.

Even though you aren't where you want to be when you find yourself with a combined state of mind, it is an enhancement from in the past. You should be excited that you are making progress and keep up the hard work. Continue to track your progress and purposefully have a development frame of mind to step away from your set method of thinking totally.

Recap

When it comes to obstacles, perception can make or break you. Though it is simple to have a repaired mindset, a development frame of mind will assist you to overcome any obstacle and change it into success. Track your progress, show a development mindset in your vision, and stay optimistic to turn your repaired thinking into chances for development.

CHAPTER 3

YOU'RE NOT IN CONTROL

In addition to frame of mind and perception, how you see control will largely determine whether you conquer your challenge. The impression that we are in control is mostly to blame for many of the obstacles we find ourselves dealing with, but the barrier is illusionary.

Primarily, we have to acknowledge that we are not as in as much control as we would like. As people, we naturally desire control over our entire lives. Regardless of this strong desire to be in control, we are only in control of extremely little.

By trying to manage things that are completely out of our realm of control, numerous obstacles feel frustrating and daunting. That's because they are. Seeing ourselves as in control creates numerous fabricated barriers that we have no chance of getting rid of. It is important to learn this lesson if you are to conquer obstacles.

Understanding When To Let Go

Because of this control issue, a number of us hang on to barriers that we have no organization holding onto. These will be obstacles that we have no chance of getting rid of. Whenever we try to overcome challenges that we can't beat, we get overwhelmed and blame ourselves. More than likely, your failure to conquer a barrier has nothing to do with you but the truths of the matter.

With this in mind, it is necessary to bear in mind that you must not get caught up in things that are not in your control. Concentrating on things beyond your control loses your time and energy, and it might harm your self-esteem. Just concentrate on matters that you have at least partial control over.

Whenever you find yourself dealing with a barrier that you aren't sure if you should control, you may wish to evaluate it. If you can not manage the barrier result in any way, let go of it. Understanding whether you must release can be difficult, but there are two things to consider:

1. The truths
2. Your feelings

The truths of the barrier and your feelings will figure out whether you are in control of the result and if you must release it. The facts of the barrier consist of anything that is a requirement for the barrier to be overcome.

For example, state your challenge is that you have been fired and need money. The realities would consist of the length of time you can go without an income, the number of individuals relying on you, and anything else that can be objectively determined.

In addition to the facts, you need to consider your emotions. Your feelings will mostly figure out if the challenge deserves it to you. In some cases, the challenge is in your control, and the realities allow you to conquer it.

However, your feelings might tell you that the barrier is not worth it. Let's look at an example. Assume that your partner gets a new job and must cross the country. The challenge in front of you is whether or not you ought to move or remain in a long-term relationship.

Both of these options are workable, however, your emotions might inform you that you don't wish to move and you can't tolerate a long-distance relationship. Because of the case, your emotions tell you that this barrier is not worth it and that you need to possibly separate.

By taking a look at the realities and your emotions, you must be able to figure out if a barrier deserves it. If the challenge is not, provide it up and proceed with your life. Though this may take a great deal of strength and strength, it will make your life much easier.

How to Let Go of Control

To carry on, you need to acknowledge and release control. For the majority of people, this can be hard. Here are some valuable action steps to help you release control and get back to living a life you take pleasure in.

Focus on What You Can Control

The initial step to letting go of control is to focus on what you can manage and recognize what you can't. What you can control just associates with you, and the list is very small. Your appearance, mindfulness, elements of your health, and productivity are examples of things that are within your control.

Any situation that includes another person is not totally in your control. You can manage how you react to the other person, but you can not control how they act or the scenario.

Notice Your Response Pattern

Your response pattern is how you respond to another individual or circumstance. The majority of the time, our feelings result in our reactions. This isn't always bad, but it can imply that you respond badly, which harms your ability to overcome the challenge.

Notice your reaction pattern to alter the outcome. Your response pattern will include the trigger, stress response, unfavorable thought, negative feeling, reactive habits, and the repercussion. Take a second to assess this reaction pattern so that you know how you respond.

If you believe that your response is poor and causing bad consequences, you need to break the pattern. This involves observing the trigger, breathing, and being thoughtful to yourself and others throughout the procedure.

Also, turn your negative idea into a more practical one. Changing your reaction pattern will offer you much more control over yourself. Still, it won't entirely alter the scenario, however, it will help how you react to it and your sensations.

Mantras

You can also use mantras to help release the control freak inside you Mantras fast and helpful expressions that you recite to yourself throughout the day. Studies have shown that mantras work if you repeat them to yourself often.

They alter the way you believe, and for that reason, they alter the way you. react. Here is a list of helpful mantras for releasing control:

- I let go of the need to control others.
- I release anything beyond my control.
- I control myself and my happiness.
- I only manage myself and my responses.

Recap

Our need for control turns things that we should let go of into obstacles. Discover how to identify when obstacles are not worth your time. Then, work to let go of your requirement to control everything to get back to your life and just deal with barriers that are worth your time.

CHAPTER 4

IDENTIFYING OBSTACLES

Now that we have set the stage for overcoming challenges, we can dig into how to turn them into success. Just like any other obstacle that may come with your method, the initial step to conquering your barrier is to determine it. To put it another way, you need to know what the challenge is and classify it.

Recognizing the obstacle will make you more aware of the positives, negatives, your own biases, and what you require to do to conquer it. If you don't recognize your barrier, it will be impossible to come up with action steps to follow. Though there are many barriers, lots of could be classified into bigger groups, such as facing the unknown or minimal finances.

In this chapter, we are going to take a look at the most typical categories for challenges. You may observe that the obstacle in front of you is a mix of more than one classification. That is completely normal. Let's take a look at what these typical barrier types are.

Facing the Unknown

One of the most basic challenge types is facing the unknown. Facing the unknown is whenever you find yourself in a circumstance that is unknown territory. Whenever you move, get a brand-new task, or talk with a new person, you could find yourself dealing with the unknown.

This challenge will be extremely difficult for those with anxiety, introverted characters, and low self-confidence. That's because it takes a great deal of courage and confidence to overcome this challenge and make the unknown familiar.

The best way to conquer this barrier is to remind yourself that everyone has remained in a comparable scenario in the past, and most people are not going to judge you. Also, deal with your self-confidence to become more trusting of yourself and your capability to act in the unknown.

The pressure to be Someone Besides Yourself

Another challenge you might face is pressure to be someone besides yourself. This pressure can originate from family, pals, or society. Some individuals struggle with this barrier more than others. Ladies particularly face this challenge, but males do as well.

To conquer this obstacle, you require to understand where to fix a limit between yourself and others. What are your worths? What do you think about yourself? What do you desire out of life? Asking these sorts of concerns will clarify where you end, and other people start.

To face this challenge, you require to deal with limit setting. As soon as you draw the line and create an extreme limit between yourself and others, you have to have the guts and determination to follow through. You might need to deal with your self-esteem and self-esteem to maintain the borders.

Restricted Finances

Restricted finances are an extremely tough obstacle. In numerous situations, restricted financial resources are due to something outside of your control. Losing a task, welcoming a new member to the family, an unexpected mishap, and more can all result in a minimal monetary obstacle.

Unlike the last two barriers, this one will need far more tangible and conclusive action steps. This includes producing a budget plan, understanding just how much more cash you require to make, and more. It might likewise need you to search for a new job or ask for a partner to assist economically.

In addition to the apparent issues that come with limited finances, such as not paying costs, there will also be other challenges that you have to deal with, such as strained relationships, facing the unknown, and more.

Relationship Issues

Relationships are among the most frequent locations for barriers. As human beings, we are all entitled to our ideas and actions, but we frequently feel that everyone ought to fall in line with our ideas. As a result, a great deal of stress can be produced, and it is harder to conquer these challenges considering that it includes another fully autonomous person.

Frequently, a barrier in a relationship is a particular occasion or pattern. To determine the challenge, you require to talk with the other person to identify their side of the story. Deal with the other individual to develop action steps to remove the challenge in the future.

In some cases, the barrier may be irreconcilable. For instance, your partner may not desire kids while you do. Frequently, the only method for overcoming this barrier is separating and finding a brand-new partner with the same objective and desire for children as you.

You can also have challenges associating with problems with your good friends, moms, and dads, or kids, not simply your romantic partner. Approach their resolution in the same manner.

What to Do After Determining the Challenge

Once you determine the challenge, it is essential to develop action steps that are directly connected to the issue at hand. Action steps offer you something concrete to do to conquer the barrier. Your action steps should not be too lofty, however, they must rather be more like mini-goals. We will talk more about this in the next chapter.

In addition to action steps, you might require to reflect on yourself. Particular obstacles will take a big toll on your psychological and psychological well-being. Reflect on yourself and focus on your feelings. Lots of people are lured to put their feelings aside to get rid of the challenge rapidly.

Completely disregarding your feelings is just as hazardous as getting swept away by them. Consider your emotions and utilize them as directions for learning. Depending on where you stand emotionally, you might wish to speak within a self-help book or see a therapist to overcome the problems.

More times than you would believe, the genuine barrier lies between your ears, not in the real world. Make the effort to reflect upon yourself, your goals, and your desires to come to a firm understanding of where you stand.

Recap

The initial step to overcoming the obstacle is to identify the precise problem. You can do this by breaking up the barrier into classifications, which will assist the barrier to see more tangible in your mind. From there, create action steps and touch back into your emotions to pursue a resolution actively.

CHAPITRE 5

SET GOALS

As we pointed out in the last chapter, goals are an essential way to get rid of challenges and transform them into success. Objectives are more difficult than you may think, though. Many people are clueless about goal development and follow-through, making it challenging to conquer obstacles.

In this chapter, we are going to look at how you ought to set up objectives to overcome your obstacles. These goals can be called SMART goals. Let's have a look.

SMART Objectives

The best type of objectives to set is called SMART goals. SMART is an acronym for specific, quantifiable, achievable, practical, and prompt. Incorporating all 5 of these aspects into your objectives makes sure that they are manageable which you are capable of accomplishing.

A specific goal is one that has one intention in mind. It needs to be exceptionally focused so that you have a particular concept of what you need to achieve. More than that, the specific objective needs to be measurable. This indicates that you require to be able to measure whether or not you attained the goal.

On top of that, it needs to be both possible and reasonable. There is no point in setting an objective that you can not achieve or that is entirely outside of your capabilities. Finally, set a time frame by which you need to accomplish the objective. This will keep you motivated.

For example, say that the challenge in front of you is that you need to reduce weight. The goal ought to be to lose 25 pounds in 3 months. This weight loss goal of 25 pounds specifies, quantifiable, possible, realistic, and prompt.

What If I Can't Come up With a SMART Objective?

State that you have been thinking of a SMART goal and keep coming up with nothing. If you find yourself in this situation, you can ask a buddy or relative for guidance. They may have the ability to give you a brand-new point of view that you hadn't considered.

If you still aren't able to come up with a SMART goal, then the chances are that you do not have control of the scenario. If you do not have control over it, then there is no chance to set a goal to achieve it. You can set goals to relieve symptoms of the barrier, but you can't guarantee success.

You may encounter this issue if your obstacle involves another person. Say your partner wishes to leave you, and you don't want a divorce. Considering that there is another equally autonomous individual included, you don't have complete control over the circumstance. As a result, you may not have the ability to set SMART objectives to ensure success in the scenario.

However, you can create SMART goals to assist you to survive the procedure or relate to your partner better. Talk through the scenario with your partner to try to get on the same page. From there, set goals to reduce the blow. This may involve counseling, focusing on your hobbies, or something else that you have control over.

Follow Through

Your objectives are nothing if you do not follow through with them. When you set your goals, discover a method to motivate yourself to keep operating at them. SMART objectives are the best way to keep up and stay motivated. Even with SMART goals, nevertheless, you have to keep working.

You might want to create benefits on your own after breaking up the SMART objective into smaller-sized goals or mini-goals. Every time you reach a mini-goal, you reward yourself. This keeps you thrilled and ready to fulfill the next mini-goal.

Devote yourself. Many individuals set goals, but they don't commit to them. Ensure that you follow through by not giving yourself the chance to slack. Just as you would hold someone else accountable for fulfilling their commitments, hold yourself accountable also.

Be Flexible

When discussing objectives, we would be amiss not to mention versatility. When many people set objectives, they are very rigid and declined to flex. This is practically a guaranteed method to fail and not overcome your challenge. Rather, you need to be versatile, even when it pertains to goals.

Sometimes, plans modification, challenge modifications, or your priorities change. When this happens, you need to have the ability to move your focus and objectives to reflect this event. If not, the objectives will be disconnected from where you are in life. Too stiff goals are bound to break ultimately.

Instead of viewing goals as something stiff, view them as fluid. Be rigid in following through with your goals but want to change them if you need to. Whenever the plans modify, versatile objectives will flex with the pressure instead of breaking.

Recap

Objectives help you accomplish your obstacles. Set SMART objectives to keep you inspired and most likely to turn your challenges into success. Though you will need to commit to yourself and hold yourself responsible, goals are truly the only method not to get damaged by your obstacles.

CHAPTER 6

<u>FOCUS ON YOURSELF</u>

We can not talk about overcoming challenges without discussing the importance of concentrating on ourselves and not comparing ourselves to others. Because of social media and many other factors today, it is simpler than ever to compare yourself to somebody else.

Doing this is destructive to our development, success, and wellbeing. Not to mention, it makes conquering challenges almost difficult and puts brand-new obstacles in our lap. To overcome barriers, you need to break this routine instantly. Your whole health and wellness will change for the better.

Though it is easy to compare yourself to others when dealing with a barrier, you need to prevent it.

Why You Shouldn't Compare Yourself to Others

The primary reason you should not compare yourself to others when conquering any challenge is to produce more barriers at the same time. Simply put, it makes a mountain out of a molehill. If you are already stressed about the primary obstacle, you do not wish to make the process any more difficult than it has to be.

Furthermore, comparing yourself to others might impede your ability to live the life you desire. When you compare yourself to someone else, you are seeing yourself and them through their perspective. Doing so indicates that you aren't valuing your opinions and ideas as extremely as you should.

If you continue to worth somebody else's ideals above your own, it might be difficult to overcome a barrier or produce the life you want. Just focus on yourself and stop comparing yourself to others to prevent this from taking place.

Comparing Yourself to Others Develops Unrealistic Concepts

There are a couple of reasons why comparing yourself is not only bad but impractical. Most notably, you never get the whole picture when taking a look at somebody from the exterior. Individuals like to appear better off than they are, so they just show the silver linings.

When you compare yourself to others, you are comparing yourself to an unrealistic standard. You aren't seeing the difficulties, barriers, or difficulties they had to face to get to where they are. This leaves you with an unrealistic understanding of where you should be.

Another reason why comparing yourself to others is impractical is that it simply is not relevant to you. Even if you might get the whole picture, which you can't, it's not your life. To invest your energy in comparing yourself to others is a complete waste of time.

What Should You Do Rather?

Instead of comparing yourself to others, you should contemplate your desires and desires. This will provide you a strong concept about where you are and where you wish to be. It is the most useful and reasonable method of overcoming any obstacle.

If you need to compare yourself to anyone, compare your current self to your previous self. You need to have grown by now, and the truth you are taking a lot of effort to break your relative ties reveals that you have enhanced. Compare yourself to your previous self to further growth.

It is OK to talk to other people and get their guidance. Other people have been through comparable scenarios as you. Talk with them to find out what they say about the circumstance. Don't take their advice blindly, though. Compare it to your ideas and wants and go from there.

How to Stop Comparing Yourself to Others

Here are some ways to stop comparing yourself to others:

Know Your Triggers

Know your triggers, which are things that make you feel insufficient and lead you to compare yourself to others. Triggers might be specific individuals on social media or entering into specific shops. Know your triggers, so you understand when you are likely to compare yourself to others.

Once you understand where your triggers are, try your finest to prevent them. This may be difficult, however, it is highly essential-- Unfollow people who make you feel bad about yourself or prevent locations that cause you to compare.

Remember You Don't See the Whole Story

Whenever you find yourself slipping up, keep in mind that you don't see the whole story. People will put on a front to make themselves seem much better than they feel. Remind yourself of this reality to assist bring you back to a more reasonable understanding.

Be Grateful for Your Life

Lastly, find methods to reveal more thankfulness on your own in your own life. Look at every single thing you love about your present life and repeat it to yourself. As you're making a list, you'll most likely find way more things to like than you initially thought.

If extreme contrast is something you deal with, you may wish to begin your morning or end your day with this suggestion. You will soon find yourself more grateful for your own life and self.

Recap

It is extremely easy to compare yourself to others whenever you are dealing with challenges, but you should fight this urge. Comparing yourself to others is damaging to overcoming barriers, and it is entirely impractical. Make a mindful effort to stop comparing yourself to others to open more success.

CHAPTER 7

LET'S TALK ABOUT EMOTIONAL RESILIENCE

Whenever you deal with any difficulty, it is incredibly easy to get swept away by your feelings and feel hopeless. When this happens, it can be next to difficult to get rid of the obstacle at hand. One way to neutralize these emotions is through emotional resilience.

What is Emotional Durability?

Psychological strength is a skill for soothing yourself whenever you find yourself dealing with an unfavorable experience. This unfavorable experience can be your own emotions, a challenge, or anything else that causes your mind and emotions to run widespread.

Everyone is born with a bit of psychological strength. That is how we are all naturally able to handle a minimum of some hard events. The older we get, our emotional durability deepens, permitting us to handle a lot more difficult situations.

You can even intentionally improve your emotional durability through practices, self-compassion, and self-confidence. Improving your psychological resilience will assist you to get rid of any challenge that comes with your method. It might be practical to think about emotional strength like a muscle. All healthy human beings are born with muscles. As we grow, our muscles grow too.

Some people even put in the time to exercise and target specific muscles to grow as strong as possible. Whenever we find ourselves required to lift something or impress a possible date, we might flex our muscles. To put it simply, we utilize our muscles all the time, but we can bend them whenever we desire.

Our emotional resilience is the same way. Psychological durability assists us throughout the day, however, it may be needed more so during individual events.

How Does Emotional Resilience Assist You Overcome Barriers?

Psychological resilience is essential for not simply conquering obstacles however changing them into success. It is only through psychological strength that we feel we can deal with difficulties and improve on our life. This is an important element of getting rid of barriers that you can't neglect.

Let's imagine a life in which you had no psychological resilience. You may rapidly give up, cry, and get down on yourself because of the barrier. You aren't able to manage your mind or emotions, inhibiting you from getting rid of the obstacle.

However, with emotional strength, you would be able to peaceful your mind and rationally talk to yourself. This ability would then assist you to consider rational techniques for conquering the obstacle to change it into success.

Aspects of Emotional Durability

The great part about emotional resilience is that you can develop it. Whether you are very mentally resistant or not, you can always discover a bit more. In general, emotional resilience includes three elements: the physical components, psychological elements, and social components. You must focus on all components to improve your psychological resilience.

Physical aspects include your energy, health, and vitality. If you are sick and your body doesn't work as it should, it is much tougher to be mentally resilient. If you don't currently, concentrate on consuming excellent nutritious meals and getting some exercise to assist improve your emotional strength.

The mental elements include your self-confidence, self-esteem, adjustability, emotional awareness, focus, self-expression, and reasoning abilities. These aspects are vital to having good emotional resilience. You will require to do a lot of individual work to target this component, depending on your specific requirements.

For example, you might have a problem with self-confidence but be great in your reasoning capabilities. If that's the case, you may wish to go to a therapist to talk through the reasons that you feel adversely about yourself. Other individuals may have the opposite problem. They may have terrific self-esteem but low thinking abilities. Those individuals may wish to begin finding out more to challenge their brains.

Finally, the third component is social components. This is your interpersonal relationships, interaction capabilities, and cooperation. Human beings are not created to be lone creatures. Boost your psychological resilience by deepening your connections and communication abilities with others. They will be found helpful whenever you deal with an obstacle.

Structure Psychological Strength

Whenever you want to construct your psychological durability, it is best to resolve the three aspects above. Some individuals may need aid with the relationship element however be fantastic with the other two. Reflect on yourself to learn which aspects you may need to enhance. The majority of people need to enhance all three to some degree.

From there, you need to be watchful about your ideas and actions. Notification whenever you feel bad about yourself or whenever you feel like you lose control. As you are noticing your ideas and actions, practice talking yourself down and self-compassion.

Talking yourself down involves unwinding your ideas. See if there are any contradictions or logical factors that come to your mind. Unmasking these thoughts will assist you to come to a lot more level-minded location. In addition to focusing on yourself, make the effort to deepen your relationships. This might be as simple as setting up a lunch with your moms and dad, but it might also be as extensive as requesting help from a buddy.

You might even want to discuss what you've been finding in your mission for self-reflection while deepening your social relationships. If you are finding building your psychological durability to be exceptionally tough, consider speaking to a therapist or licensed expert. These specialists will help you determine your problem ideas and unwind them to increase your emotional durability.

Recap

Psychological resilience is essential to overcome any barrier. Much like a muscle, your psychological strength can be grown through deliberate thoughts and actions. Even if you are currently emotionally resilient, continue to develop this muscle to help transform any barrier into success.

CHAPTER 8

TURN CHALLENGES INTO SUCCESS

Lastly, we have reached the last chapter of this book. Up until now, we have spoken about the fact about obstacles and how perception and the false illusion of control mainly determine your ability to conquer them. We've likewise discussed determining obstacles, setting objectives, concentrating on yourself, and emotional strength to help you find a way through your challenge.

But how do you transform a challenge into success? After all, merely overcoming the challenge isn't like prospering. In this chapter, we're going to give you essential ideas not just to overcome your barrier but change it into an effective symbol of success in your life.

Practice, Practice, Practice

As the old stating goes, practice makes ideal. To beat any challenge that comes your way, you have to have practice in conquering them. This indicates that transforming barriers into success might be tough initially, but it will get much easier as you go. This is a natural reality about life.

Practice all of the suggestions above every time you face a challenge, no matter how small the obstacle may seem. Consider this as barrier strength training. This training will help you get into the practice of getting rid of barriers to finding out exactly what you need to deal with within yourself.

If you don't feel like you have any barriers to practice on, you probably aren't looking hard enough. Obstacles are so common in our life that the majority of them go undetected. Take a crucial take a look at your daily life, and you will likely find a challenge or two concealing there.

Don't Quit

Some challenges will be more difficult than others. Make sure not to give up. Even if you feel stuck and like the method isn't working, continue standing firm. Only through continuous effort can you transform challenges into success. Of course, this isn't the same as letting go when it's not worth it. If your gut is telling you that you should not be worrying a lot over a certain subject, then listen to it.

But do not quit simply because the difficulty is hard, or you are frightened. Giving up out of worry will only hurt you. Plus, you will likely regret it in the future, and life's too short to regret any actions!

Stay Optimistic

One of the very best ways to ensure that you don't quit is to remain positive. As we already discussed, there is constantly a minimum of one positive to any obstacle you face. Keep these favorable in your mind's eye to remain optimistic.

In addition to remaining positive about the challenges you deal with, stay positive about yourself too. If you feel that you deal with self-confidence or self-respect, talk to your physician. These are extremely important concerns that require to be resolved.

Stay positive about your life as a whole too. Even if you aren't exactly where you want to be yet, acknowledge that you are closer to reaching your goal than ever before. This will assist you to stay thrilled about facing your challenges given that you are already so near your end goal.

You're Not In The Clear Yet

As soon as you overcome the barrier at hand, it might be tempting to breathe a sigh of relief and believe you are in the clear. Though you must certainly commemorate and get excited about conquering your barrier, you are not in the clear yet.

As we have stated sometimes throughout this book, barriers are all over. Even if you overcome one does not imply that it will be smooth cruising from here on out. Soon, another obstacle will come your way.

Be prepared for upcoming obstacles by continuing to push yourself, even when you don't feel like it. This might appear extreme, but this continual pursuit of improvement is what will transform your barriers into success. Focus on yourself and your enhancement, even when the challenge is over.

Recap

The only way to transform a challenge into success is to integrate what you have gained from this book into your daily life. While you face a challenge and overcome it, continue to practice and push yourself to utilize these techniques. Just then will you see a genuine change internally, which will allow you to succeed elsewhere in your life?

CONCLUSION

Barriers are an unavoidable part of life, however, they can be extremely difficult. Undoubtedly, discovering to overcome a challenge might put you under a great deal of social or financial strain. On top of that, barriers challenge your emotional and psychological mastery, causing some to crack under pressure.

Nevertheless, with a little bit of effort and intentionality, you can conquer obstacles and change them into success. Simply by acknowledging that there are positives to challenges which your understanding matters, you mainly take away a lot of the power of obstacles.

Moreover, acknowledging that you are not in complete control minimizes the number of barriers you can face. From there, you can approach any challenge with a level of mind and a bit of rationality. This enables you to determine challenges and set objectives for an active follow-through. As you are attempting to accomplish your goals, concentrate on yourself and construct your emotional resilience. Just by doing this, you are practically guaranteed to get rid of any obstacle.

The true procedure of success is how the barrier impacts you and forces you to grow. The only way you can transform the obstacle into success is by implanting the lessons found out into your mind and improving your life.

Continue to practice, remain optimistic, and enhance yourself to turn any obstacle into a chance for success truly. I'm going to caution you. The journey is not going to be simple. There are going to be times when you want to give up and believe that all your effort is worthless. It is at those times when you need to stay motivated and thrilled one of the most. Keep your chin up, and you are going to be turning barriers into success in no time.

Printed in Great Britain
by Amazon